# MY LIFE PARTNER

# KEYS TO A HEALTHY MARRIAGE

**GIDEON O. STEPHEN**

# TABLE OF CONTENTS

# INTRODUCTION

Most people enter relationships without fully understanding what makes a marriage happy and successful. There are a lot of things to think about when choosing a life partner, like the person's upbringing. Also, partners have profound effects on one another. The process of choosing a life partner is simple, but when people use questionable methods, they make it more difficult. Before a friendship can develop into a relationship, it is necessary to identify a friend to ascertain whether or not potential partners share some aspects of life. If the relationship is successful, it leads to marriage.

This method does not involve free-choice mate selection, in which two people fall in love and get married because they are attracted to one another by instinct. Choosing a life partner necessitates a deep love and understanding of one another as well as an understanding of what each partner wants in their lives. While some people marry out of luck, others do so out of lust or self-esteem, they all hope for a happy union.

People get married for the wrong reasons in modern society. For instance, one might be compelled to get married by society so that they don't face the stigma of getting older alone. At 40, being single is more stigmatized by society than being in a troubled marriage at the same age. The single person may not be far from a happy marriage, but troubled couples end up in chaos or divorce for the rest of their lives.

A careful process of selecting a life partner necessitates commitment and understanding on the part of both parties. Marriages and relationships face challenges, but they can be overcome if partners know what they want.

# CHAPTER ONE
# CONCEPT OF MARRIAGE

## Meaning of Marriage

We frequently hear the term "marriage" in our daily lives. Have you ever seriously considered it? What does marriage entail? Is it just a man and woman's relationship to live together and have children? Is it a creation of man? When was the establishment of such an organization? The responses to the aforementioned questions, particularly those regarding the meaning, scope, purpose, and history of marriage, will be particularly fascinating to consider.

For different people, the term "marriage" has different connotations and meanings. Marriage, according to some, is a union between men and women for human evolution. Some view it as a permit for sexual activity. Marriage is viewed as a means of companionship by another group. Marriage encompasses all of these perspectives and more. It is an extremely complicated institution that cannot be described in a few sentences.

Regarding the significance and scope of marriage, a great number of philosophers and sociologists have held opposing views. Marriage is a man-made custom or institution that dates back to prehistoric times, but it is not intrinsic to human nature. It is a conscious commitment made by a man and a woman, not a natural relationship. Marriage became a social institution with religious and legal backing as civilization advanced.

Civil or religious marriage is a legally binding union between two people (a man and a woman) who intend to live together as sexual and domestic partners. Marriage, also known as matrimony or wedlock, is a culturally accepted union between people who are called spouses. It establishes rights and responsibilities between the people, their children, and the laws of their country. The bonding of two people through a social union or legal contract typically based on a sexual relationship and requiring a permanent union could also be referred to as marriage.

Like family, marriage is a cultural institution that can take many forms. Who gets married, what it means for the couple and society as a whole, why people get married (for love, economic, political, or other reasons), and how it happens (wedding or other ceremonies) are all very different in different societies. Variations should also be taken into consideration when practicing cultural relativism; such as whether more than two people can be involved (think polygamy) or whether a legal union is required (think "common law," marriage, and its equivalents). Whether spouses are of the same sex or different sexes, as well as how the traditional expectations of marriage (to produce children) are understood today, could be other variations on the definition of marriage.

As a result, different cultures have their take on marriage, which is why there is such a wide range of definitions of the term. It has changed over time, both in terms of who is included and what is not. Although marriage is a well-known concept that has existed since ancient societies, it has not always been what modern society considers it to be. There are a variety of reasons why people get married. Social, economic, religious, emotional, or legal reasons are all examples of these. Because it is a custom that has been handed down to us from previous generations, we in the modern era appear to instantly link love to marriage.

Marriage, as previously stated, has distinct connotations and meanings. Let's examine a few of them.

## Marriage as Relationship

Marriage is one of the most satisfying and profound human relationships. It has existed in various forms throughout human history, responding to each generation's fundamental needs and social aspirations.

## Marriage as an Institution

The institution of marriage is the union of a man and a woman, their bodies, minds, and souls, as well as their feelings and aspirations. Love is at the heart of this union. Because it is a personal relationship between the partners, marriage is regarded as the primary relationship. Marriage is beautifully explained by Lin Yutan. He asserts, "Man is clay, the woman is water, and the clay holds the water and gives it substance in which the water moves, lives, and has its full being."

## The Biological Aspect of Marriage

Man marries, whereas animals mate. We can say that marriage is a social event while mating is a biological process from a biological perspective. One of the fundamental instincts for reproduction is the sex instinct. However, in the case of man, this instinct has been subject to distinct regulations and control since the beginning of society. The regulation and control of biological reproduction can be described as a marriage. Because there is no society or social norm in the animal kingdom, there are no clear rules for mating. However, there are a variety of social restrictions, religious restrictions, and even marriage laws in human society. Sex relationships between humans are permissible within certain parameters. Marriage is a lifelong, sanctifying, loving union between a man and a woman that leads to the birth of children.

## The Social Aspects of Marriage

We have seen that marriage has more social aspects than biological ones. However, there are some biological aspects to it. In human society, these social facets hold the greatest significance. Love is the most important factor in marriage. When a man and a woman marry, true love means giving everything to one another. The minds and souls ought to join together. Emotions and wills ought to coexist. All of these imply self-giving that is complete, exclusive and lasts a lifetime.

## The Psychological Side of Marriage

Marriage is a necessary component of human existence. The fundamental longing of man for completeness and communication reaches its logical conclusion in marriage. Both men and women find fulfillment in life. The process by which two people who want a more perfect life give themselves completely to each other is called marriage. Male and female partners complement one another in a marriage. If a person is on their own, it fills the physical and mental void that they have. Marriage makes it possible to satisfy the male and female's strong and natural desire to be in the union that nature has designed for them.

## The Legal Aspect of Marriage

A man and woman's union must be legal. Therefore, marriage ought to be accepted by society, law, and civil society. The prevailing social norms and practices determine whether marriage is legal. It differs from society to society. Only those who are capable of performing the fundamental act of marriage can legally contract the marriage.

# CHAPTER TWO

## THE FUNCTIONS AND PURPOSES OF MARRIAGE

Have you ever wondered why two people should get married? The spread of the human species, perhaps, is the first response that comes to mind. Let's try to figure it out.

**Marriage for Union and Reproduction**

What exactly is marriage for? Marriage is not necessary if the sole purpose is to conceive. Union and procreation are among the most important purposes of marriage. Marriage is a physical, psychological, and spiritual means of communicating love and self-commitment.

**Marriage for Sex**

Conceiving children is the natural end of a sexual relationship. As a result, having children is an essential goal of marriage. The union itself—the love, pleasure, and contentment of the husband and wife—is an equally significant goal. As a result, marriage fosters love and attachment between partners. It makes it possible to express sexual satisfaction lawfully.

**Marriage for Companionship and Friendship**

The most fundamental need of a person is the intimacy that comes from sharing a home with and committing to another person. How does friendship work? "Friendship is having a privileged position in someone else's life and giving them a privileged position in our own," says Jennet Kid. Sharing ourselves with people we like, is it? Marriage is built on friendship, which endures even after the sexual desire has passed. Even after the children have grown up and settled down, it remains. It only gets worse over time. This is what friendship and companionship mean. It makes a man or woman a better person by making them more selfless and enhancing their capacity for love and sacrifice. Therefore, marriage is essentially companionship or friendship, as well as sex, family, and love.

### Marriage for Socialization

Marriage is a way for a person to reach their full potential in terms of socialization and development. It offers numerous opportunities to foster love, cooperation, and security. To provide a natural environment in which a person can realize themselves and reach out to others with an attitude of dedication and service, a family is another purpose of marriage. It gives society a solid foundation and children a safe place to grow.

### Marriage for Mature Relationships

Another reason to get married is to become more mature by having relationships with other people. Marriage also serves the purpose of raising and educating children. The relationship between a parent and their child is one of closeness.

### The Financial Requirements of Marriage Partners Are Met

The framework for meeting people's needs is provided by marriage: food, clothing, safety, and other necessities people know for whom they are financially and socially responsible through the marriage institution.

### Marriage Keeps Families Together

This is related to the previous function, but marriage legitimately enables people to learn about inheritance rather than simply knowing who is with whom socially and economically.

**The care and enculturation of children are institutionalized by marriage.**

Children learn about their gender roles and other cultural norms during marriage. Marriage establishes who is in charge of the children. By socially establishing their birthright, it legitimizes children.

# CHAPTER THREE

## FACTORS THAT MAKE MARRIAGE WORK

Individuals and couples can experience feelings of dissatisfaction, unhappiness, and unfulfillment in their marriages or relationships at times, and they may be unsure of the exact cause.

Numerous factors contribute to a satisfying marriage or relationship, such as;

**1. Love/Commitment.**

Love is fundamentally a decision to commit oneself to another. It is much more than a fleeting feeling that is depicted in romance novels, movies, and television. Healthy marriages are characterized by a genuine decision to be committed, which endures indefinitely.

Marriage is a decision that must be made through both good and bad times. Commitment is simple when conditions are favorable. However, true love is demonstrated by remaining committed throughout life's challenges.

**2. Sexual Fidelity.**

In marriage, sexual devotion extends beyond our bodies. Our eyes, minds, hearts, and souls are also included. Sexual fidelity to our spouse is sacrificed when we focus on fantasies about another person. Sexual faithfulness to our spouse is sacrificed when we offer emotional intimacies to another person.

Protect your sexuality daily and give it all to your partner. Being sexually committed necessitates self-control and awareness of the consequences. Put nothing in front of your eyes, heart, or body that would make you less faithful.

**3. Humility.**

Everyone has flaws, and relationships always show these flaws more quickly than anything else. The capacity to acknowledge that you are not perfect, that you will make mistakes, and that you will require forgiveness is an essential component of a healthy marriage. Resentment will develop and your relationship will not progress if you maintain a sense of superiority over your partner.

Take a pen and paper and quickly write down three things that your partner does better than you if you struggle in this area. This simple exercise should help you remain humble. As often as necessary, repeat.

**4. Patience/Forgiveness.**

In a marriage, patience and forgiveness will always be required because no one is perfect. Couples who have a happy marriage learn to forgive and be patient with one another without ceasing. They humbly acknowledge their shortcomings and do not expect their partner to be perfect. They do not attempt to hold their partner hostage by bringing up previous mistakes.

In addition, when mistakes are made, they do not seek retribution or amends. Forgive your partner if he or she has hurt you in the past and you are holding onto that. It will liberate both your heart and your relationship.

**5. Time.**

Without investing time, relationships fail. Never have been, never will be. For a relationship to be successful, it is necessary to spend time together in a meaningful way. And when there is insufficient time, quality time rarely occurs.

The most intimate and substantial relationship you have should be with your spouse. It will therefore take longer to develop than any other relationship. Make time each day for your spouse if you can. A once-in-a-while date night wouldn't hurt either.

**6. Trust and Openness.**

In a happy marriage, trust and honesty become the foundation for everything. However, unlike the majority of the other essentials on this list, trust develops over time. While selflessness, commitment, and patience can all be developed quickly, trust always takes time. After weeks, months, and even years of being who you say you are and doing what you say you will do, trust is built. Start now because it will take time, and if you need to reestablish trust in your relationship, you will need to put in even more effort.

**7. Communication.**

Partners in a happy marriage communicate frequently. They talk about the schedules of the kids, grocery lists, and utility bills. However, they do not end there. Additionally, they convey hopes, dreams, and anxieties. Not only do they talk about the changes in the child's life, but they also talk about the changes in their hearts and souls.

Sincere and forthright communication serves as the foundation for so many other aspects of this list, so it is impossible to ignore this crucial factor: a few examples include patience, trust, and commitment.

**8. Selflessness.**

Even though it will never appear in any survey, selfishness is the leading cause of divorce. Money, infidelity, incompatibility, or incompatibilities are all blamed in surveys, but most of these factors stem from selfishness. The self-centered person is only committed to them, has little patience, and never learns how to be a good spouse. Give your partner your life, hopes, and dreams. And begin a life of shared experiences.

This is a straightforward plea to cherish our marriages, care for them, and regularly invest in them.

If you want to learn how to have a happy marriage, the aforementioned marriage advice will always require nearly every part of you. However, it is so worth it.

The majority of the temporal things we pursue in our lives are less valuable than a happy and successful marriage. And will always be more durable.

# CHAPTER FOUR

## CHARACTERISTICS OF A LIFE PARTNER

One of the most important characteristics of a good partner is that they share a strong emotional connection with you.

You and your spouse have a deep connection when you have an emotional intimacy or interpersonal relationship. You may even have a spiritual connection and feel admiration, love, and romance for each other.

You can do the following when you are emotionally close to your spouse:

1. Be open and honest in your communication with your partner. Spending time together builds emotional intimacy. Be vulnerable without fear of being judged. Feel at ease in silence with your partner.
   Trust each other without hesitation.
2. They exhibit physical affection
   Most people believe that a healthy relationship requires physical affection. Touch builds sexual chemistry and makes us feel loved by our partners. The ability to be affectionate without all the sex is one of the best qualities in an ideal partner.

   Not only do you benefit from a physically affectionate partner, but you also have a strong sexual connection. The simple act of holding hands, cuddling on the couch, or even receiving a massage from your partner can increase relationship satisfaction.

3. They show you respect
   Love is more than just how warm and happy you feel around your partner; however, respect is one of the most important characteristics of a good spouse.

   All of your emotional, sexual, and physical boundaries will be respected by your partner if they respect you.

   What exactly are these boundaries?

   a. Limitations of emotion: These are the things that make you feel at ease and secure in your relationship. If your partner treats you with emotional respect, it means that they won't intentionally hurt your feelings. They are helpful and kind to you.
   b. Limits of sexuality: What you want and don't want to do in bed is respected by your partner. They won't try to coerce you into doing something you don't want to do or make you do it.
   c. Limits imposed by nature: You should never be hit by your partner. They won't hurt you in any way if they respect your physical boundaries. This includes all forms of physical abuse, from assaulting you to uncomfortably grabbing your wrist.

   Respectfulness is one of the most important characteristics of a good partner. And if you've discovered one, never let it go!

4. They demonstrate unwavering devotion
   One of the best qualities of a good partner is their unwavering devotion to their partner.

   You will experience feelings of insecurity if your partner is unfaithful. Jealousy, suspicion, and heartbreak will become commonplace when you are with someone you know you can't trust.

On the other hand, being in a committed relationship will leave you feeling loved and fulfilled.

Being in a committed relationship has the following advantages:

a. Establishing a solid foundation for your future: If you are confident in your partner's ability to commit, you won't be afraid to get involved in more significant activities like marriage, moving in together, or starting a family.
b. Safer sex: When you're in a committed relationship, your chances of getting an STI from your partner are much lower.
c. You won't have to worry about arguments: Any time you get into a fight, you won't have to worry about breaking up. You can rest assured that your partner will always have your back, even when you disagree with each other.

You are content because commitment lessens the drama in a relationship. You won't have to worry about where your partner is or who they're with when you are happily committed to monogamous love.

5. Beautiful couples openly communicate outdoors in love.

What Makes a Good Spouse?

According to the Journal of Marriage and Family, couples' communication predicts marital satisfaction. Happier couples communicate with one another more frequently.

Small disagreements can be avoided by communicating with one another.

Couples can work through problems calmly and respectfully when they are open and honest about their feelings.

However, communication is about more than just resolving conflicts; it is also about sharing stories, aspirations, and objectives.

When you talk to one another:

Find out what your partner needs and say what you want. Grow closer emotionally. Be honest. Make your partner feel special. Break bad habits. The more a couple of talks to each other, the deeper their relationship gets. Therefore, open communication is one of the most important qualities of a good partner.

6. They are your best friend: Although romantic relationships are wonderful, you shouldn't want to be in one all the time.

   The foundation of friendship is one of the most important characteristics of a good partner.

   Strong evidence suggests that best friends make couples happier. “Life satisfaction" was found to be "twice as large for those whose spouse is also their best friend," according to a study that was published in The Journal of Happiness Studies.

   You and your friend play games, talk and laugh together. This is great for your relationship because studies have shown that laughing together makes couples feel more supported and content.

   A strong friendship is a key to a happy relationship. It ensures that your partnership has both the romance and sexual chemistry of a relationship and the fun and flair of a friendship.

7. They have great sexual chemistry with you: One of the most important qualities of a good partner is that they have great sexual chemistry with you.

Physical intimacy not only causes the bonding hormone oxytocin to be released, but it also makes you feel wanted, boosts your confidence, and builds a special connection with your partner.

When it comes to having an amazing sex life, communication will be your best friend. You should be able to talk about boundaries with your partner, explore your fantasies, and express your needs in the bedroom.

Another advantage: Both men and women reported higher levels of contentment and orgasm frequency when there was more sexual communication, according to studies.

Someone who respects you in the bedroom and cares about your needs is a great partner. It doesn't hurt to have great sexual chemistry as well!

8. They give you their full attention: It's one of the most reassuring qualities to look for in a person to have this quality.

   If you're trying to talk to your spouse while they're playing on their phone, there's nothing more frustrating.

   Multitaskers were subjected to MRI scans in a study that was published by the University of Sussex. People who spend a lot of time using multiple devices (texting and talking, using a tablet while watching television, etc.) lacked empathy and emotional control more than people who concentrate on a single thing at a time.

   Someone who won't be afraid to put their phone down and give you their full attention is one of the most important qualities to look for in a partner. They will set aside time for you to talk, are good listeners, and won't interrupt you while you're talking.

9. Romantic Mixed-Race Affectionate: Young newlyweds relax at modern hotel interior while viewing foreign country on vacation. One of the most important characteristics of a good partner is their belief in mutual trust.

   When two people in a relationship:

   They are reliable build emotional intimacy extends trust to you. Mutual trust and honesty are essential qualities in a relationship. They are true to their word. They know how to communicate their issues. They can admit when they are wrong and apologize for it.

10. They practice forgiveness: Being able to practice forgiveness is one of the best qualities of a good partner.

    One of the most difficult things you will ever have to do is forgive someone who has deeply hurt you.

    Many of us tend to forgive our partners only to forget about what went wrong and later remind them of how they hurt us. That is not genuine repentance.

    Real forgiveness entails:

    Getting to the bottom of why it happened, discussing the issue, accepting your spouse's genuine apology, determining whether or not you can forgive the wrong, repairing and strengthening your relationship, forgiving the matter, and not bringing it up again. Acknowledging the hurt and processing the betrayal. Carefully considering how you are affected by your partner's decision. Discussing the issue. Getting to the bottom of why it happened.

The best qualities in a partner are love and trust. Relationships are all about growth. Love, forgiveness, communication skills, friendship, trust, commitment, and sexual and emotional chemistry are among the most admirable characteristics of a person.

The qualities of an ideal partner listed above are not a "do or die" list. If your partner does not possess all of the aforementioned desirable personality traits, don't worry about it.

Remember: Even if your partner doesn't yet possess all of the qualities that make a good partner, that doesn't mean they won't develop into the kind of person you want to be with throughout your relationship.

# CHAPTER FIVE

## HOW TO CHOOSE A LIFE PARTNER

It is truly empowering and exciting to choose the person or type of person with whom you want to spend the rest of your life. You should use both your head and your heart to make the right decision. Being in love with someone is very important, but you should also think about some practical things because you want to spend the rest of your life with them. Don't worry; we've compiled some pointers to assist you in determining the kind of person who is best suited to you.

### PRIORITIES IN YOUR RELATIONSHIPS

- **Choose your ideal way of life.**

This is a big decision, but fortunately, once you start spending a lot of time with your partner, you usually know pretty quickly what they want out of life. In terms of how you want to spend your spare time, how you want to interact with your friends, and the kinds of material comforts you want to pursue, you and your partner should share similar ideas. You don't have to agree with your partner on everything, but you shouldn't disagree on matters that call for major decisions or commitments.

For instance, a couple that has one partner who enjoys simultaneously watching nature documentaries and pro wrestling on Monday nights will probably be able to work things out (especially if they agree to buy a DVR). However, major obstacles to long-term happiness include when one partner wants to buy a house but the other does not, or when one partner wants to be a "swinger" but the other does not.

❖ **Choose where you would like to live.**

Sometimes, a couple's happiness depends on where they live. People often want to live near close friends or relatives or in areas where certain kinds of activities can be done. At the very least, it may be necessary for both partners to travel a lot if they are unable to live happily together.

❖ **Make up your mind about having children.**

This is a hugely significant choice, possibly the most significant one you and your partner will ever make. Despite this, a surprising number of couples fail to adequately discuss it before attempting to commit to a long-term relationship. Raising a child can be the most rewarding thing you ever do, but it also comes with a lot of responsibility, a lot of money, and the decision to spend at least 18 years (or more) directly responsible for your child's care. As a result, it should not be taken lightly.

Don't make assumptions about your partner until you know for sure. The majority of people in the United States want children, but this is not necessarily the case everywhere.

❖ **Consider the significance of your religion and culture to you.**

Some people are agnostic or atheist and have little non-mainstream culture or tradition, while others is heavily influenced by their cultural or religious traditions. While both lifestyles have merit, some partners may find that a partner on the opposite end of the spectrum is not a good long-term choice. It's important, to be honest about whether or not your partner needs to be like you in this area of life before you commit to someone.

To be clear, people of all races, religions, and cultures can happily marry for the rest of their lives. For instance, there are now more interracial couples than ever before in the United States.

❖ **Choose how you'll use your money.**

Although discussing money can be awkward, two life partners need to be on the same page about it. Money can have a significant impact on how a couple's life unfolds—it can dictate how long each member of the couple works, the kinds of jobs they take, the lifestyle they can lead, and more. Anyone considering a long-term relationship should openly discuss how they intend to save and spend money together.

Consider the following as an illustration of the kinds of financial decisions that couples must make: Both partners may not be able to get their way in a couple where one partner wants to spend his late 20s and early 30s traveling a lot and learning about the world, while the other wants to build a successful career and save for a house.

Throughout our lives, our families influence our thoughts and actions. If you want to spend the rest of your life with someone else, you must have a clear idea of how you want them to fit into your family. You'll want to know what role you want your partner to play in both your immediate family (you and any children you have) and your extended family (parents, siblings, cousins, etc.).On the other hand, you should let your partner know how to do this.

For instance, it is crucial for some couples with children for one parent to take care of the children full-time. Others are fine with a nanny filling in. Similarly, some individuals may desire more independence while others may prefer to live close to their parents and visit them frequently.

## COMPATIBILITY

- **During the beginning stages of a relationship, ask a lot of questions.**

Talk to a new person about who they are as you meet them and start dating them. Find out what they value most in a partner, their life objectives, and their plans for the future. Don't be afraid to inquire about your partner's ethics, interests, spiritual outlook, and even diet—all of which may be crucial to your long-term compatibility!

In all aspects of your lifestyle choices, you will need to think about questions. Take, for instance, how you both feel about money. Do they have any potential issues from the past? Will they be understanding and supportive if you want to change careers or advance?

To be clear, you shouldn't always ask these kinds of questions on your first date. If you ask someone very personal questions early on, it can be a big turnoff and hurt your efforts to start a relationship. However, you will probably want an answer to these major lifestyle questions within, say, the first six months of your relationship.

- **Utilize your past relationships' experiences.**

Think back to the relationships you've had in the past if you're having trouble deciding what you want in a partner or life. Whether you are conscious of it or not, the choices you make in your relationships can help you figure out what you want in a partner and what you might need to work on to make a long-term relationship work. Some examples of questions you might want to ask about your previous relationships are as follows:

What was your partner's best quality?

What were your favorite things to do together?

What caused you and your partner to disagree?

What was the reason you criticized your partner?

What was the reason your partner criticized you?

What was the reason for the breakup?

- **Set goals for your life.**

For almost all of life's major decisions, if not all of them, two people spending their lives together need to be on the same page. Even if two people get along perfectly otherwise, a disagreement over a significant, non-negotiable aspect of your life can end a relationship in its tracks. Try not to lie to yourself because doing so can result in long-term resentment and is unfair to your partner. Be open and honest about these goals. Before you choose your life partner, here are a few very important questions you should know the answers to:

Do I desire children?

Where would I like to reside?

Do I prefer to manage my home or work?

Do I want to be the only one in my relationship?

What goals do I have for the future?

What kind of way of life do I want?

- **Have a true understanding of who you are.**

You are the first step on the path to finding a life partner! You need to know who you are to choose the best person for you. Know your strengths and weaknesses, as well as your strengths and weaknesses.

Know exactly what you want from life and your partner. Be sincere and realistic with yourself. Try asking your closest friends for help if you're having trouble examining yourself.

Most importantly, love yourself regardless of your flaws. You can't expect someone else to love you if you can't love yourself. If you try to have a relationship for the rest of your life while you have a negative self-image, you will probably hurt the people closest to you and hurt yourself, so get this important first step in order before you continue.

## RELATIONSHIP ADVICE

- **Don't hold on to your hopes.**

Don't expect the other person to be someone they aren't when you're trying to keep a relationship going. While a couple can reach a compromise on several important issues and even alter minor aspects of them to please their partner, most people will always be the same person. Do not project any kind of illusory image of your partner or attribute qualities that they do not possess. Also, don't expect a partner to change a lot of their personality to please you. For instance, it's fine to ask your partner to start taking out the trash from time to time, politely, of course. This is a reasonable place to look for a compromise. However, it is not acceptable to anticipate your partner's sudden decision to have children if they have not already done so; this is a deeply personal choice that cannot be undone.

- **Describe who you are honestly.**

You must do the same for yourself, just as you shouldn't try to hide or change any major aspect of your partner. It can be tempting to manipulate the truth about your past or current situation to please someone you like when you are dating. However, this not only creates personal guilt but also increases the likelihood of future issues. It is perfectly acceptable to dress a little fancier than you normally would for your first few dates, but you wouldn't want to pretend that you are agnostic when you are quite religious just to make your date happy. The level of trust in the relationship can seriously suffer when the other person learns the truth. A deception that many people find difficult to overcome is lying or omitting information about them to mislead their partner about who they are.

❖ **Spend a lot of time with a person you might date.**

How can you find out if you can spend a lot of time with another person? Give it a shot! Spending a lot of time with the other person (ideally in a variety of settings) is crucial to determining whether or not a relationship will last. If you can bear to be with someone for days, weeks, or even months at a time, you might have found your soul mate.

You should probably also check to see if this person gets along with your friends and family. Participate in social events with your partner and introduce them to your family and friends. You won't have to worry about anything else if your partner gets along well with these people.

❖ **Give it some time.**

There's no need to jump right in because you're looking for a partner for the rest of your life. Allow your relationship to develop naturally. For major relationship milestones like "going steady," moving in together, and getting married, do not adhere to an arbitrary schedule. If you rush into these decisions, you run the risk of finding yourself in unanticipated situations with someone who might or might not share your priorities in life.

Until you get to know a potential partner, you should avoid getting too close to them. Sexual intimacy should not serve as the foundation for long-term happiness, even though it is certainly possible to transform a causal relationship into something more serious. Waiting allows you to better understand whether you are compatible with the other person, even though sexual attraction and compatibility are essential to a successful long-term relationship.

- **Pay attention to how you behave around your partner.**

If you notice yourself acting "fake," pretending to feel something different from what you do, or laughing at things you don't find funny, this could be a sign that you don't feel at ease around this person. However, you are on the right path if you are at ease and completely at ease around the person. Being able to be completely honest with your partner is essential. You don't want this to happen to you five years into marriage because everyone eventually runs out of energy to keep "faking it."

- **Be prepared to give up some things.**

There is no perfect relationship. For the sake of your partner, you might have to put your own needs ahead of your partner's. The extent to which you are willing to make sacrifices is entirely up to you; the majority of healthy relationships involve both partners making healthy sacrifices.

When it comes to giving up little things for the sake of your relationship, things like insignificant personal habits and actions should be considered. However, major life objectives typically shouldn't be because disagreements over one of them can indicate incompatibility. If you have a spouse and children, for instance, deciding to go out drinking with your friends less frequently is a reasonable sacrifice. On the other hand, you shouldn't put yourself through making the decision not to have children when you so badly want them.

## TIPS FOR MAKING A MATCH

- **Take initiative.**

There is someone who can help almost anyone; all you have to do is look for them. The chances of finding the person who is right for you can be seriously reduced if you don't even try new things, meet new people, or leave the house. Therefore, if you want to find a life partner, the first step is to get up and leave! Spend at least some of your free time going to fun social events, meeting new people, and exploring the world around you.

The majority of "experts" in dating will advise taking a proactive dating approach. In terms of the amount of effort you should put into it, some even rank it higher than your career!

- **Meet people who are doing what you enjoy.**

You don't have to spend every Friday night in a noisy, crowded, and overpriced nightclub to meet potential dating partners, nor do you have to be a Hollywood type who is perfectly dressed and debonair. While some people find success with these methods, the majority of people will have the most success finding partners simply by participating in activities they enjoy. When you do this, you probably meet people who share your interests and outlook, which naturally leads to compatibility.

Even hobbies that are done by you can provide chances to meet new people! Do you enjoy video games and comic books? Participate in an event! Love to paint? Organize an exhibit! Like to write? Attend a workshop for writers! Start looking—there are exciting activities for almost every interest!

❖ **Be authentic.**

Since you want to spend the rest of your life with someone, it makes sense that you and your potential life partner should be completely honest about whom you are. A lot of people are reluctant to "open up" completely until they have gotten to know someone well. If you can bear the thought, try to be completely honest with yourself from the beginning of a relationship through every stage: going on your first few dates, asking someone out, getting to know each other better, committing to each other, and more! Instead of forcing your partner to "hold on" until you are at ease being who you are, you give them the chance to fall in love with the real you by doing this.

❖ **Don't be scared.**

It can appear to be a risky journey to find your life partner. Particularly if you have recently experienced romantic setbacks, it can appear as though you have almost no chance of finding the right person. Don't ever give up hope or succumb to the fear that you won't find someone, no matter what you do. People all over the world face the same kinds of romantic challenges that you might be facing at the moment. Everyone experiences personal setbacks on occasion. Don't compare yourself to other people or couples because there is no one "right way" to find a life partner. Don't let your negative thoughts get in the way of your search for a life partner. Finding the right person for you requires perseverance, bravery, and confidence!

In addition, confidence is generally regarded as quite sexy! Fearless confidence is a self-reinforcing quality that significantly increases your attractiveness to potential partners: When you approach dating situations with more confidence, you will feel more at ease, have a better time, and be more self-assured when you face the next one.

**SUMMARY OF ARTICLE**

Choosing a life partner may seem daunting, but you will have a better chance of finding someone if you know what you want, put yourself out there, and set realistic expectations. Think about what you want out of life first. For instance, do you prefer to focus on your career and travel the world rather than settle down and have children? Utilize this vision to imagine your ideal partner once you have a clear understanding of your life goals. The next step is to meet people who share your interests by joining clubs, attending social events, and browsing online dating sites. Find out how this fits into your vision by asking them about their hopes and aspirations. Even though you should find someone who wants a future similar to yours, it will be hard to find someone who fits you perfectly, so you should be willing to compromise on smaller details. Continue reading for additional advice, including how to draw lessons from previous relationships to find the ideal life partner!

www.ingramcontent.com/pod-product-compliance
Lightning Source LLC
La Vergne TN
LVHW020538160826
845677LV00015B/4136

* 9 7 9 8 3 5 7 6 2 3 7 2 0 *